1001
WAYS TO BE
KIND

Dallas Woodburn

Published by Familius LLC, www.familius.com

PO Box 1249, Reedley, CA 93654

Familius books are available at special discounts for bulk purchases, whether for sales promotions or for famil
or corporate use. For more information, contact Familius Sales at orders@familius.com. Reproduction of this
book in any manner, in whole or in part, without written permission of the publisher is prohibited.

Library of Congress Control Number: 2023941281

Print ISBN 9781641709019

EPUB ISBN 9781641708388

Kindle ISBN 9781641708371

Fixed PDF ISBN 9781641708364

Printed in China

Edited by Mikaela Sircable and Lara Carbine

Cover design by Mckay Rappleyea

Book design by Mckay Rappleyea

10 9 8 7 6 5 4 3 2 1

First Edition

Introduction

"No act of kindness, no matter how small, is ever wasted." —*Aesop*

Kindness is a cornerstone of my identity, my belief system, my faith in the world. As a newborn, my life was saved by the care of strangers whom I can never repay. I was born three months prematurely, weighing a mere 2 pounds 6 ounces, and back in the late 1980s, my chances of survival were extremely small. And yet, because of the doctors and nurses who selflessly cared for me 'round the clock for months in the NICU, I have been blessed with a healthy, happy life—and am now a mother myself.

One need not have a dramatic story to have their life changed by kindness. I believe that everyone can look back on at least one moment in their life when a caring act made a profound difference.

Kindness need not be big or showy or splashy or loud. Kindness can be quiet, easy, and gentle. Kindness can require just a few moments.

And yet, tiny acts can have enormous impact.

Tiny acts of kindness empower us to look outside ourselves, beyond our own problems and worries, and focus on what we can do to help someone else.

Tiny acts of kindness open our hearts, reminding us of the infinite ways we are all connected.

Tiny acts of kindness can change the world . . . and our lives. Not only the lives of the receivers, but of the givers, too.

A few years ago, I embarked on a Year of Kindness, performing fifty-two random acts of kindness for others. Every Monday, I wrote down a new kindness challenge for that week, and the following Monday, I journaled about my experiences and chose a new challenge. Week by week, one small act at a time, I hoped to make the world a slightly brighter and happier place.

My Year of Kindness turned out to be one of the most meaningful experiences of my life, helping me navigate a year far more personally tumultuous than I ever could have anticipated, with a broken engagement, a new job, and a solo move across the country to a brand-new city. My weekly acts of kindness were my life raft in an ocean of change, grief, and uncertainty.

I learned that being brave and putting yourself out there is worth it. Time and again, I was delighted by wonderful connections and coincidences—and by the acts of kindness that others did for me.

My hope for this book is that it fills you up with ideas, with motivation, with love. Here are 1,001 acts of kindness to encourage and energize you. Use this book as inspiration for your own kindness journey. Maybe you want to commit to a week of daily kind acts? Go for it! Or echo my Year of Kindness and pick a kind act to do every week for a year! Or team up with friends and create a kind acts scavenger hunt. Why not use random acts of kindness as a bonding exercise for your workplace, sports team, or church community? Or perhaps you would like to celebrate a special occasion like a birthday or anniversary by doing a whole bunch of kind acts all day long!

Let this book serve as a menu of ideas, organized into a variety of different categories, that you can use as a jumping-off point in your own life. Focus on one category at a time, or skip around throughout the sections as your heart pleases.

Will you join me? Together, we can all make our world a more compassionate, gentle, and beautiful place. Let's get started!

—*Dallas Woodburn*

Everyday Kindness

"How we treat one another is the only thing that matters."

—*Samite Mulondo*

1. Arrive early.
2. Text someone to let them know you're thinking of them.
3. Give a genuine compliment.
4. Write a thank-you note.
5. Do a favor for someone.
6. Hold the door open for someone.

7. Pull a chair out for someone.
8. Smile at everyone you meet.
9. Ask someone about their day, and actively listen to what they say.
10. Offer to carry something for someone.
11. When waiting at a red light, scoot over so another driver can pull up beside you and turn right.
12. Let someone go ahead of you at a four-way stop.
13. Let someone merge ahead of you on the freeway.
14. Walk quickly across a crosswalk when a car is waiting to go.
15. Let someone go ahead of you in line.
16. Pick up litter on the ground and throw it away.
17. Help someone clean up a mess.
18. Stand up and offer someone else your seat.
19. Stop to help someone who is hurt.
20. Be present.
21. Give someone your full attention.

22. Ask, "Can I help you with that?"
23. Say, "Thank you." And mean it.
24. Let someone vent, and listen without judgment.
25. Straighten up someone's mess.
26. Leave your spare change in the tip jar.
27. Surprise someone with a small gift.
28. Cook for someone.
29. Turn off all the lights when you leave a room.
30. Give hot chocolate to someone out in the cold.
31. Give ice-cold water to someone out in the heat.
32. Take care of someone who is sick.
33. Help someone who is lost.
34. Give everyone the benefit of the doubt.
35. Plant seeds.
36. Be patient.
37. Scoot over to make room for someone.
38. Invite someone to join you.
39. Extend an olive branch.

40. Be a mediator.
41. Keep your promises.
42. Ask someone else for their opinion.
43. Be polite.
44. Forgive someone.
45. Let someone help you.

Holiday Kindness

"Carry out a random act of kindness, with no expectation of reward, safe in the knowledge that one day someone might do the same for you."

—*Princess Diana*

46. New Year's Eve: Send a friend a "Happy New Year!" message when the clock turns to midnight in their time zone.
47. New Year's Day: Volunteer at a soup kitchen to serve a hot meal to others.
48. Valentine's Day: Bring Valentine treats to a nursing home.

49. Valentine's Day: Send a card to an old friend you haven't talked to in a while.
50. Valentine's Day: Give someone flowers.
51. Saint Patrick's Day: Volunteer to drive an intoxicated reveler home.
52. Saint Patrick's Day: Leave gold coin chocolates in a public place for strangers to find.
53. Tax Day: Donate a percentage of your tax refund to charity.
54. Easter: Create a fun Easter egg hunt for neighborhood children.
55. Easter: Surprise someone with an Easter basket filled with their favorite treats.
56. Earth Day: Volunteer for a beach cleanup or other cleanup of a natural habitat.
57. Earth Day: Donate to an environmental organization.

58. Arbor Day: Plant a tree in your backyard.
59. Arbor Day: Donate to arborday.org to plant a tree in someone's honor.
60. Mother's Day: Write a kind note to a mother figure in your life.
61. Mother's Day: Send a text checking in on a friend who has lost their mother.
62. Memorial Day: Leave flowers at a cemetery in remembrance of veterans who lost their lives.
63. Memorial Day: Donate to an organization that provides support to military personnel, past and present.
64. Juneteenth: Visit a museum or exhibit dedicated to Black culture.
65. Father's Day: Write a kind note to a father figure in your life.
66. Father's Day: Send a text checking in on a friend who has lost their father.

67. Fourth of July: Volunteer your time at a local event or parade.
68. Fourth of July: Bring extra earplugs to your local fireworks show and pass them out to others (especially children!).
69. Labor Day: Send a handwritten letter to a business about a salesperson who was especially helpful to you.
70. Halloween: Deliver Halloween treats to a nursing home.
71. Halloween: Decorate your house to delight the neighbors who pass by.
72. Halloween: Donate your old pumpkins to a nearby zoo to use as food for the animals.
73. Halloween: Trick or Treat for UNICEF.
74. Indigenous Peoples' Day: Learn about the tribe or tribes of native peoples that lived where you live now.

75. Indigenous Peoples' Day: Support Native artisans and display their work.
76. Veterans Day: Thank a veteran for his or her service.
77. Thanksgiving: Invite someone to your Thanksgiving dinner.
78. Thanksgiving: Give someone a ride to or from the airport.
79. Thanksgiving: Volunteer for a food bank, meal delivery, or soup kitchen.
80. Holiday season: Send a holiday greeting to say, "Thinking of you."
81. Holiday season: Help someone address their holiday cards.
82. Holiday season: At a holiday party, go talk to someone who is standing alone.
83. Holiday season: Put up decorations in your yard or window for others to enjoy.

84. Hanukkah: Take your menorah to a neighbor who doesn't have family nearby and light the candles with them.
85. Hanukkah: Invite someone to your Hanukkah celebration.
86. Christmas: Help someone put up Christmas lights or decorations.
87. Christmas: Go caroling and spread cheer.
88. Christmas: Write and send handwritten thank-you notes for your gifts.
89. Christmas: Name your tree in honor of someone you love.
90. Kwanzaa: Invite someone to join in your Kwanzaa celebration.
91. Kwanzaa: Help someone solve a problem.

Self Kindness

"Whoever is happy will make others happy too."

—Anne Frank

92. Forgive yourself for some guilt you are holding onto, and let it go.
93. Put your hands on your heart and take three deep breaths.
94. Take a long walk.
95. Give yourself permission to rest.
96. Pour out your emotions into a journal.

97. Sit outside in the sunshine and allow yourself to just *be*.
98. Delete social media apps that are depleting your energy or self-confidence.
99. Look into the mirror and say these words out loud to yourself: "I love you. You are doing a great job."
100. Name three things you are grateful for, right now in this moment.
101. Take a break.
102. Savor your favorite cup of coffee or tea. Relax and enjoy every last sip.
103. Make time to move your body.
104. Sleep in.
105. Sink into a good book.
106. Ask yourself, "What do I need right now?" Listen to the answer without judgment.

107. Write out a list of all the things you love about yourself.
108. Clear out everything from your closet that doesn't make you feel like your best, most beautiful self.
109. Take a nap.
110. Daydream.
111. Make a nourishing meal to fuel your body.
112. Be still and listen to the quiet whispers of your heart.
113. Say these words out loud to yourself: "I am enough, exactly as I am."
114. Relax with a long, hot bath.
115. Get a massage.
116. Listen to your favorite music.
117. Dance.
118. Stand up and stretch.
119. Go outside.

120. Turn your phone off for a few hours . . . or for the whole day.
121. Bake something elaborate.
122. Watch your favorite movie.
123. Relive a favorite memory.
124. Clean out and organize a messy drawer.
125. Do that one task you've been putting off so you won't have to worry about it anymore.
126. Find a photo of yourself that you love. Display it somewhere you will see it often.
127. Light a candle.
128. Are you hungry? Tired? Stiff? Listen and give your body what it needs.
129. Get a manicure or pedicure. Or get both!
130. Meditate. (Even if you only have two minutes.)
131. Order dessert.

132. Get a facial.
133. Take a long, hot shower. Use the fancy soap.
134. Take yourself out on a date.
135. Do a small task that will make your day easier tomorrow.
136. Give yourself plenty of time.
137. Give yourself plenty of grace.
138. Stand tall. Take up space.
139. Whatever you are feeling in this moment, let yourself fully feel the emotion. No shame or judgment. Just the truth of how you really feel.
140. Look at yourself in the mirror and smile.
141. Write out a list of reasons you are proud of yourself.

Family Kindness

"A kind gesture can reach a wound that only compassion can heal."

—*Steve Maraboli*

142. Give an extra-long hug.
143. Call or text a relative to say, "Good morning! Have a beautiful day!"
144. Start an impromptu family dance party.
145. Spend meaningful time with a relative you don't normally see.
146. Call a loved one on the phone.
147. Send a video message to a relative.

148. Do a family member's typical household chore without being asked.
149. Take turns going around the dinner table and saying something you are grateful for.
150. Volunteer as a family at an animal shelter or soup kitchen.
151. Choose a charity to donate to as a family.
152. Offer to drive someone where they need to go.
153. Offer to keep someone company on a long drive.
154. Help out with a family tradition.
155. Say, "I'm really proud of you."
156. Be quiet so a family member can sleep in.
157. When you're at the grocery store, pick up someone else's favorite snack or treat.
158. Compliment a family member on something new.
159. Support and share a relative's fundraising endeavor.

160. Organize a family reunion.
161. Make time for a family get together, even when you are busy.
162. Send a card to a relative just to say, "Thinking of you."
163. Listen with enthusiasm to a story you have already heard many times before.
164. Ask a relative to tell a favorite story again.
165. Tell a story highlighting a family member's strengths.
166. Learn a family recipe, and make it to share with others.
167. Write a note to your sibling that lists a bunch of reasons why you love them.
168. Help a family member with a project.
169. Reach out to a family member with a sincere apology.

170. Offer to babysit or pet-sit for a relative.
171. Create a family mantra together.
172. Create a new family tradition.
173. As a family, cook a meal for someone else.
174. Say, "I love you."
175. Make a scrapbook together of your favorite family adventures.
176. Order groceries to be delivered to a sick relative who lives far away.
177. Create a kindness jar: write kind acts you witness on slips of paper and drop them into the jar. Empty the jar and read them aloud as a family at the end of the week.

Friend Kindness

"Make friendship a fine art."

—*John Wooden*

178. Reach out to an old friend you haven't talked to in a while.
179. Mail a postcard to your friend.
180. Text your friend just to share one of your favorite qualities about them.
181. When you meet up at a café or restaurant, sneakily pay for your friend's coffee or meal.
182. Ask questions with openness and curiosity.

183. Remember details about their life.
184. Text your friend a photo of the two of you together and ask, "Remember this?"
185. Give them a print of a favorite photo of the two of you.
186. Compliment your friend.
187. Write a letter telling your friend what you admire about them.
188. Call just to check in.
189. Send a voice or video message to say, "Thinking of you!"
190. Surprise your friend with a delivery of their favorite food.
191. Send an encouraging quotation that made you think of them.
192. Celebrate your "friendiversary"—the anniversary of the day you two met.

193. Write a post on social media sharing how wonderful they are.
194. When you're out and about, pick up a small gift that made you think of your friend.
195. Drop off dinner at your friend's house when they are sick or stressed out.
196. Offer to help your friend with an annoying task they've been putting off.
197. Invite your friend to come to an event with you.
198. Listen without judgment or advice. Just listen.
199. Make time for your friend in your schedule.
200. Be present. Put your phone away and give your friend your full attention.
201. Send your friend a funny meme that you know will make them laugh.
202. Give your friend a handmade gift you created just for them.

203. Remember important dates in your friend's life—happy and sad anniversaries—and reach out with extra love on those occasions.
204. Celebrate your friend's successes. Pop the champagne!
205. Keep your friend's favorite drink in your fridge or snack in your pantry to make them feel extra welcome when they come over.
206. Surprise your friend with flowers or produce from your garden.
207. Drive your friend to an appointment so they don't have to go alone.
208. Offer to babysit so your friend can rest and recharge.
209. Stick up for your friend.
210. Remind them of all the reasons why they are awesome.
211. Be a plus-one to an event your friend is dreading.

12. Make a donation to a cause that your friend believes in.

13. Give your friend a homemade card.

14. Save them a seat.

15. Offer to lend your friend something they need.

16. Give them a copy of a book you think they'll like.

17. Instead of giving back your friend's empty food container, fill it up with a treat you made.

18. When you meet up for a walk, bring an extra water and snack for your friend.

19. Slip a kind note into your friend's wallet or purse.

20. Reach out to apologize.

21. Wish a friend well on a new adventure.

Relationship Kindness

"Go and love someone exactly as they are. And then watch how quickly they transform into the greatest, truest version of themselves. When one feels seen and appreciated in their own essence, one is instantly empowered."

—*Wes Angelozzi*

222. Give them the last bite.
223. Give them a foot rub.
224. Let them set the thermostat.
225. Let them hold the remote.

226. Give a long hug.
227. Try to see things from their perspective.
228. Leave a loving note on their pillow.
229. Fill up their tank with gas.
230. Wash their car.
231. Plug in their cell phone if it is low on charge.
232. Share a list of reasons why you love them.
233. Text to say, "I appreciate you."
234. Take a chore off their plate.
235. Leave an encouraging note on the bathroom mirror.
236. Put away their laundry.
237. Make their morning cup of coffee or tea.
238. When they tell you about their day, be present and listen.
239. Hold their hand.
240. Rub their back.

241. Pick up medicine when they are sick.
242. Sing their praises.
243. Ask, "Is there anything you need?"
244. Text a favorite photo of the two of you.
245. Celebrate their achievements.
246. Let them pick the restaurant for date night.
247. When walking in the rain together, let them hog the umbrella.
248. Ask questions about their hobbies.
249. Do their favorite activity together, even if it's not your cup of tea.
250. Surprise them with their favorite dessert.
251. Give them flowers.
252. Load the dishwasher.
253. Empty the dishwasher.
254. Call in the middle of the day just to say, "I was thinking of you."

255. Take them breakfast in bed.

256. Listen without judgment.

257. Help with a task that makes them anxious.

258. Give them space to cry.

259. Listen to their dreams.

260. Be the first one to apologize after an argument.

261. Don't hold grudges.

262. Kiss them hello.

263. Kiss them goodbye.

264. Surprise them with a kiss just to say, "I love you."

265. Remember important dates in their life, even from before you two met.

Kind Acts for Adults to Do for Children

"When I was young, I used to admire intelligent people; as I grow older, I admire kind people."

—*Abraham Joshua Heschel*

266. Scatter lucky pennies around a playground.
267. Give a child a penny to throw into a fountain at a mall or park to make a wish.
268. Greet them with a warm smile.

269. Instead of saying, "Hurry up!" let them dawdle and daydream.

270. Turn your phone off and put it away so you can give your full attention to play.

271. Bake a cake together and let them pour and stir.

272. Take three deep, centering breaths together.

273. Ask, "What do you think?" And really listen.

274. Surprise them with a trip to the park.

275. At the grocery store, buy a balloon and leave it with the cashier to give to a child who passes through the checkout line.

276. Stop at a child's lemonade stand, even if you're not thirsty, and leave a big tip.

277. Fly a kite together.

278. Listen and ask questions as they tell you all the details about their favorite book, movie, or TV show.

279. Let them choose what music to listen to in the car.
280. Let them choose what movie to watch.
281. After bath time, surprise them with a warm towel just out of the dryer.
282. Give a big, long hug.
283. Hold their hand.
284. Read an extra story at bedtime.
285. Read the same book over and over, as many times as they request.
286. Play their favorite game over and over without complaint.
287. Say, "I'm so proud of you."
288. Play outside together.
289. Let them get really, really messy.
290. Forgive a mistake.
291. Make up a special song together.

292. Display their artwork.
293. When they give you a gift, wear or use it often.
294. Let them order for themselves in a restaurant.
295. Give them stickers just because.
296. Take them out for their favorite dessert.
297. Leave a note on their bathroom mirror that says, "You are amazing!"
298. Leave an encouraging note in their school lunchbox.
299. Drive them to school or the bus stop instead of making them walk in the rain.
300. Ask for their opinion.
301. Write them a letter describing all the wonderful things about them.
302. Look through their baby album together and tell them stories about when they were first born.

303. Hold space and sit with them in their big emotions instead of trying to brush aside their feelings.
304. Make a scavenger hunt.
305. Make up your own secret code that means, "I love you."
306. Give them a kiss, even if they pretend to be annoyed.
307. Help them work through a problem on their own.
308. Crochet them a special hat or blanket with love in every stitch.
309. Write them a story where they are the hero.
310. Decorate their bedroom with streamers and balloons.
311. Be encouraging and curious about their unique interests.

312. Remember all their friends' names.
313. If they ask you for a favor, say, "I'd be happy to!"
314. Celebrate their effort even more than their achievement.
315. Say, "It's okay. It was an accident."
316. Help them clean up a mess.
317. Go splashing together in rain puddles (even if it means soaking your shoes!).
318. Draw a hopscotch game with chalk on the sidewalk for children to use.
319. Volunteer to coach a youth sports team.
320. Bring water and snacks to a local youth sports game.
321. Buy an extra box of Girl Scout cookies and give it to the Girl Scouts selling the cookies for them to enjoy.

322. Volunteer as a mentor.
323. Scatter tokens all around an arcade.
324. Leave quarters on a jukebox, pinball game, or gumball machine.
325. Give them a do-over if they make a mistake.

Kind Acts for Children to Do

"There are three ways to ultimate success: The first way is to be kind. The second way is to be kind. The third way is to be kind."

—Fred Rogers

326. Pick out a toy, ball, or book to donate to another child.
327. Sell lemonade and give the proceeds to charity.
328. Color a special picture to mail to a friend or family member.
329. Say, "Thank you."

330. Paint rocks with vibrant colors and leave them around town for others to find.
331. Share toys with others.
332. Wave hello to another child when you're out and about.
333. Make a surprise treat to give to a friend.
334. Send kind and loving thoughts to someone.
335. Plant a flower garden.
336. Weed someone else's garden.
337. Water plants.
338. Clean up your toys and books.
339. Buy a copy of your favorite book to donate to your school or library.
340. Fold up a nice note or drawing and slip it in between the pages of a library book for the next reader to find.

341. Pack up your outgrown clothes and toys to give to a younger child who could use them.
342. Put change in a vending machine.
343. Share your snack with someone.
344. Do a chore for someone.
345. Clean up your room without being asked.
346. Donate coloring books and crayons to a children's hospital.
347. Write a thank-you note to your teacher that describes your favorite things about them.
348. Sharpen all the pencils in your classroom.
349. Give someone a high five.
350. After it rains, bring towels to the playground and dry off the slides.
351. Sell cookies and donate the money to charity.
352. Invite someone to sit with you at lunch.

353. Be the first one to apologize.
354. Call a grandparent and ask them about their childhood.
355. Set the table with extra care.
356. Use both sides of the paper when you are coloring or drawing.
357. Let someone go ahead of you in line.
358. Let someone take an extra turn or do-over.
359. Use your inside voice when you are inside.
360. Bring someone a glass of water.
361. Give the bus driver an ice-cold soda or iced tea.
362. Stand up for someone.
363. Invite another child to play with you at the park.
364. Read a book to a younger child or to a pet.
365. Play fetch with a dog.
366. Take care of an animal.

367. Patiently teach someone how to do something.
368. Leave a care package on a friend's doorstep when they are sick.
369. Sing a song.
370. Tell a silly joke.
371. Laugh at someone's silly joke.
372. Be gentle.
373. Let someone borrow something of yours.
374. Make a comic book for your friend where they are the star of the story.
375. Bring bubbles for everyone in your class to play with at recess.
376. Pass out stickers to other children at the grocery store or waiting in line.
377. Write kind messages in your driveway in sidewalk chalk.

378. Record a video message to send to a friend or family member who lives far away.
379. Say "Yes!" instead of "No."
380. Wait for someone else to finish speaking.
381. Help your teacher or coach gather up the balls and sports equipment.
382. Instead of birthday gifts, ask for donations to your favorite charity.
383. Give your tickets to someone else to buy a prize at an arcade.

Kind Acts to Do for the Elderly

"The words of kindness are more healing to a drooping heart than balm or honey."

—Sarah Fielding

384. Bring over lemonade and enjoy a nice talk.
385. Rake leaves in their yard.
386. Weed their garden.
387. Shovel their driveway.
388. Share leftovers.
389. Invite them over for dinner.
390. Speak loudly and clearly so they can hear you.

391. Ask them questions with genuine curiosity.
392. Listen to their stories.
393. Help them with household chores.
394. Set up their computer or cell phone, and patiently teach them how to use it.
395. Learn a craft activity together.
396. Play dominoes or cards.
397. Be gracious and understanding.
398. Go for a walk together.
399. Walk slowly and carefully.
400. Take them out to a restaurant.
401. Offer to drive them around town for errands.
402. Offer to drive them to medical appointments.
403. Send a handmade card in the mail.
404. Call to say good morning.
405. Call to say good night.

406. Bring them small portions of freezer meals.
407. Take them out for a special coffee, ice cream, or smoothie treat.
408. Hold their hand.
409. Paint their nails.
410. Take them to get their hair done.
411. Give them your seat on public transportation or in a waiting room.
412. Help them stand up or sit down.
413. Listen to their advice.
414. Look through old photo albums together.
415. Wash their windows.
416. Vacuum their carpet.
417. Help them put new sheets on their bed.
418. Gently rub their back.
419. Stop in for a visit with their favorite dessert.

420. Joyfully share news and stories from your life.
421. Call them on the phone just to say hi.
422. Offer to dispose of their old prescription medicines.
423. Help them sort through old possessions they wish to donate.
424. Bring them a copy of a new book you loved and discuss it together.
425. Surprise them with a new book of crossword puzzles.
426. Watch an old movie together.
427. Joyfully listen to stories about their life.
428. Send a grocery delivery or meal service.

Kind Acts to Do for New Parents

"We find greater lightness & ease in our lives as we increasingly care for ourselves & other beings."

—*Sharon Salzberg*

429. Bring over a hot meal or organize a meal train.
430. Text to say, "Thinking of you. No need to reply!"
431. Offer to watch the baby while Mom or Dad takes a nap or showers.
432. Stop by with groceries or send a grocery delivery.
433. Do a household chore like dishes or laundry.
434. Call to check in.

435. Ask how they are doing, not only how the baby is doing.
436. Make them a care package with a few of their favorite things.
437. Gift them an audiobook they can listen to during late-night feedings.
438. Offer to watch an older sibling for a few hours.
439. Send a surprise gift of diapers and wipes.
440. Bring over a meal or groceries a few months after the baby is born, not only in the first few weeks.
441. Invite Mom or Dad to an outing with the baby.
442. Invite Mom or Dad to an outing without the baby.
443. Offer to babysit so the new parents can enjoy a date night.
444. Send a text message to tell them, "You're doing a great job!"

Kind Acts to Do for Those Who Are Grieving

"Too often we underestimate the power of a touch, a smile, a kind word, a listening ear, an honest compliment, or the smallest act of caring, all of which have the potential to turn a life around."

—Leo Buscaglia

445. Reach out to say, "I'm thinking of you."
446. Stop by with a hot meal.
447. Organize a meal train.

448. Mail a sympathy card.
449. Listen.
450. Hold space for them to feel all of their emotions.
451. Make a donation in honor of their loved one.
452. Send them a care package with a few of their favorite things.
453. Send them a book of poetry or meditations on grief.
454. Send flowers.
455. Text to check in.
456. Take them out to lunch or to the movies.
457. Do a household chore for them, like dishes or laundry.
458. Offer to watch their children or pets to give them some time alone.
459. Let them cry. Or not cry.
460. Say, "I'm here for you."
461. Say, "It's okay if you want to talk about it. Or not talk about it."

462. Offer to go along to an event or appointment they are dreading.

463. Continue checking in as the weeks and months go by.

464. Plan a special day trip to take them away from normal life.

465. Call to say good night.

466. Make them a special quilt, blanket, or scarf.

467. Offer to drive them to a grief group or support group.

468. Send flowers or a card on the anniversary of their loss.

469. Plant a tree to commemorate who they lost.

Kind Acts to Do in the Morning

"How beautiful a day can be, when kindness touches it!"

—*George Elliston*

470. Pull open the drapes and send loving thoughts out into the world.
471. Give someone a good morning hug.
472. Wake someone up with a kiss.
473. Surprise someone with breakfast in bed.
474. Make coffee or tea for someone.
475. Give someone a foot rub.
476. Text someone, "Good morning! Have a wonderful day!"

177. Call someone to say, "Good morning."
178. Take the dog out for a leisurely walk.
179. Take a neighbor's trash barrels out to the curb.
180. Bring a neighbor's newspaper up to their front porch.
181. Compliment someone's outfit.
182. Compliment yourself in the mirror.
183. Cook someone breakfast.
184. Pack someone lunch.
185. Slip a kind note into someone's packed lunch.
186. Help someone get ready for school or work.
187. Let someone else use the bathroom first.
188. Take someone out for breakfast, your treat.
189. Pay for a stranger's coffee order.
190. Send kind thoughts to the morning commuters
      around you.

Kind Acts to Do on Your Lunch Break

"Ask yourself: Have you been kind today? Make kindness your daily modus operandi and change your world."

—Annie Lennox

491. Ask a coworker if you can bring them back some lunch.
492. Put money in a parking meter that is about to run out.

493. Hold the door open for someone.
494. Offer your seat or table to someone else.
495. Invite a stranger to sit with you.
496. Compliment a person waiting in line beside you.
497. Choose to sit on the side of the table that is looking into the sun so your lunchtime companion does not have to.
498. Go up to the restaurant owner or person working the front counter and compliment the food and service.
499. Clean off your table after you are done eating.
500. Clean off another table that has been left messy.
501. Thank your waiter or waitress by name.
502. Leave a big tip.
503. Pay for the person behind you in line.
504. Buy an extra meal as takeout and give it to a homeless person.

505. Bring treats back with you to the office for your coworkers.

506. Order a nice lunch and drop it off for your child's teacher.

507. Send a nice text to a friend saying, "Thinking of you!"

508. Make a quick call to check in on someone who is sick.

509. Give your change to someone performing on the street.

510. Leave lucky pennies on the ledge of a fountain for future wishers to find.

511. Let someone else take the close parking spot.

Kind Acts to Do at Night

"Be kind whenever possible. It is always possible."

—*The 14th Dalai Lama*

512. Let a car go ahead of you while commuting home through traffic.
513. Leave the porch light on for someone coming home in the dark.
514. Walk someone out to their car.
515. Bring someone dinner.
516. Invite someone to join you for dinner.
517. Pay for someone else's dinner or drink order.
518. Cook a special dinner for someone.

519. Take your neighbor's trash barrels in.
520. Volunteer to do the dishes.
521. Let someone else choose what to watch on TV.
522. Call a friend or family member to say good night.
523. Read an extra bedtime story.
524. Give an extra-long goodnight hug.
525. Step outside and say goodnight to the moon.
526. Give someone a good night kiss.
527. Reflect on all you are grateful for from the day.

Workplace Kindness

"The best way to find yourself is to lose yourself in the service of others."

—*Mahatma Gandhi*

528. Advocate for someone.
529. Be a mentor.
530. Clean the microwave in the shared kitchen.
531. Surprise a coworker with coffee.
532. Invite the new person to lunch.
533. Use headphones so you don't distract others around you.

534. Gratefully acknowledge a coworker's contributions.
535. Volunteer to take notes for a meeting.
536. Remember your coworkers' birthdays.
537. Pair constructive feedback with genuine compliments.
538. Stay late to help out on a project.
539. Water a coworker's plants when they are on vacation.
540. Check in on a coworker who is out sick.
541. Organize a group card or gift for a coworker who is celebrating a milestone like getting married or having a baby.
542. Celebrate Administrative Professionals' Day with a thoughtful card or gift to show your gratitude.
543. Take your boss out to lunch on National Boss's Day.
544. Write your boss a heartfelt email telling them why you appreciate them.

545. Write a note to a coworker you admire.
546. Ask a coworker if there is anything you can do to help make their job easier.
547. Leave homemade muffins or treats in the break room as a surprise for your coworkers.
548. Bring in extra produce from your garden to share with your coworkers.
549. Donate to a charity in a coworker's name.
550. Send an email to tell someone, "You did a really great job."
551. Go support a coworker at an event outside of work, such as a community theater production, art show, or musical performance.
552. Offer to do a favor.
553. Nominate a coworker for an award.
554. Give credit where credit is due.
555. Ask your coworkers about their families.

556. Support the endeavors of your coworkers' children. (Girl Scout cookies, anyone?)
557. Celebrate others' achievements.
558. Put change in the office vending machine.
559. Be polite.
560. Send a condolence card when someone has experienced a loss.
561. Send a congratulations card when someone is celebrating news.
562. Organize a special gift for a coworker's retirement.
563. Ask, "Are you doing okay?" And really listen to the answer.
564. Surprise a coworker with a little gift that made you think of them.
565. Set out a candy dish at your desk for people who stop by.
566. Refill someone else's candy dish.

567. Park far away to leave the close parking spots for someone else.

568. At a work conference, sit and eat a meal with someone who is alone.

569. Give a coworker the benefit of the doubt.

School
Kindness

"Each of us is born with a box of matches inside us but we can't strike them all by ourselves."

—*Laura Esquivel*

570. Write a handwritten note to thank a teacher who has impacted your life.
571. Donate school supplies like pencils, markers, and paper.
572. Donate classroom safety supplies like sanitation wipes and tissues.
573. Volunteer to help out in the classroom.

574. Volunteer to tutor a student who is struggling.
575. Contact the principal to let them know about the way a teacher went above and beyond.
576. Write a letter to your local school board supporting and praising teachers.
577. Write a letter to your city or state representatives advocating for better school funding.
578. Write a letter to the editor of your local newspaper about a school program that is doing amazing things in your community.
579. Write a post on social media about a teacher who made a difference in your life.
580. Donate books to the school library.
581. Surprise a teacher with coffee or tea.
582. Ask, "How can I help?"
583. Greet the office workers and custodial staff by name.

584. Donate sports balls for PE.

585. Drop off baked goods to the teachers' lounge.

586. Surprise a teacher with flowers and a note to say, "Thank you!"

587. Donate computer equipment.

588. Buy a teacher a gift card or ask for their wish list.

589. Put together a gift basket with pretty soaps and hand sanitizer for the staff restroom.

590. Pay a school fee or field trip fee for a student who cannot afford it.

591. Volunteer to chaperone the school dance or field trip.

592. Buy extra tickets to the school play or band performance, and give them away.

593. Bring water bottles or Gatorade for the student-athletes at a sports competition.

594. Offer to carpool with a student who lives nearby.

595. Nominate a teacher for an award.
596. Surprise a teacher with a gift card to a nice restaurant.
597. Organize a classroom gift where each student writes a short note about why they appreciate their teacher.
598. Bring holiday gifts for the custodial staff, office staff, librarian, and groundskeeper.
599. Pick up any litter you notice on the school campus and throw it away.
600. Help a teacher push in all the chairs and tidy the classroom.
601. Donate old dresses and costumes to the drama department.
602. Donate your old prom dress to an organization like Becca's Closet or Operation PROM.
603. Donate art supplies to the art department.

604. Offer to pay a child's lunch debt.

605. Sponsor or donate to a student's college scholarship fund.

606. Bid on something at a school auction or art show that nobody else has bid on yet.

607. Join the parent-teacher association (PTA).

608. Deliver a nice lunch to a teacher, principal, school librarian, or staff member.

609. Speak positively to other parents about teachers and schools.

610. Offer to plant and help maintain a school garden on campus.

611. If you work for a company or organization that allows people to come do a site tour or visit, reach out to a local school and ask if they would be interested in a field trip.

12. Contact your local high school career center and volunteer to come speak to students about your career experience.

13. Volunteer as an usher or ticket seller for a school production or musical performance.

14. Work the concessions stand at a school sports game.

Environmental Kindness

"A single act of kindness throws out roots in all directions, and the roots spring up and make new trees.

—*Amelia Earhart*

615. Plant a garden.
616. Use a reusable water bottle.
617. Turn off the faucet while you brush your teeth.
618. Recycle cans, jars, and bottles.
619. Buy glass containers instead of plastic ones.
620. Sign up to receive paperless statements whenever possible.

621. Pay your bills online to reduce your paper consumption.
622. Save old envelopes and scraps of paper to use for notes and grocery lists.
623. Use both sides of a sheet of paper before recycling it.
624. Cut down on food waste by planning out meals in advance and shopping with a list.
625. Bring a bucket into the shower to catch water, and use it to water your garden.
626. Compost your food scraps.
627. Eat vegetarian once a week (or more!).
628. Save wrapping paper and gift bags to use again when wrapping new gifts.
629. Avoid plastic food packaging as much as possible by taking advantage of bulk bins.
630. Snip the plastic rings around soda cans before throwing them away.

631. Organize a beach cleanup.
632. Dispose of your batteries, old electronics, and paint cans at a Household Hazardous Waste center.
633. Buy rechargeable batteries instead of single-use ones.
634. Save plastic bags to reuse as trash bags or litter bags.
635. Use beeswax wrap instead of plastic wrap.
636. Carpool with a friend or coworker.
637. Challenge yourself to take a shorter shower.
638. Turn off the lights when you leave the room.
639. Invest in energy-efficient lightbulbs.
640. Buy energy-efficient appliances.
641. Wash your laundry on the cold cycle.
642. Buy eco-friendly laundry detergent.
643. Ride your bike instead of driving.
644. Take the bus instead of driving by yourself.
645. Bring reusable grocery bags to the store.

546. Go for a hike or walk, and pick up any litter you spot along the way.
547. Opt for reef-friendly sunscreen.
548. Fix a leaky faucet.
549. Set your thermostat to 68 degrees Fahrenheit to conserve energy.
550. Run your dishwasher and laundry machines during off-peak hours to help conserve your community's energy resources.
551. Buy eco-friendly cleaning products.
552. Before throwing an item in the trash, take a moment to ask yourself if it can be reused or repurposed in some way.
553. Give away or donate old furniture instead of hauling it away to the landfill.
554. Go thrift shopping instead of buying new clothes.

655. Use a microfiber-catching laundry bag or install a microplastic-filter attachment to your washing machine.
656. Plant a pollinator garden with native plants.
657. Provide pollinator nesting habitats. Leave some plant stems, twigs, stumps, and leaves to remain where they fall in your yard so insect pollinators can use them for shelter and bees can use them to nest.
658. Avoid pesticide use.
659. Choose native plants for your garden.
660. Give a live plant instead of cut flowers in a bouquet.
661. Buy organic fruits and vegetables.
662. Buy recycled paper goods.
663. Use cloth napkins.
664. Use dishcloths instead of paper towels.
665. Put a small bag in your car to collect recycling when you're out and about.

566. Bring your own reusable mug to a coffee shop.
567. Ask for your water or soda without a straw.
568. Only take what you need.
569. Go on a bird-watching walk together.
570. When hiking, stay on the trail to avoid disturbing native habitats.
571. When visiting the beach, stay off the sand dunes.
572. Donate to the Rainforest Climate Action Fund.
573. Become a citizen scientist, volunteering to help professional scientists collect and analyze data in the natural world.
574. Refill water jugs or use a Brita pitcher instead of buying bottled water.

Animal Kindness

"Wherever there is a human being, there is an opportunity for a kindness."

—*Lucius Annaeus Seneca*

675. Take your dog on an extra-long walk.
676. Build a special box castle for your cat to play in.
677. Play fetch with a dog.
678. Play "chase the laser" with a cat.
679. Make homemade treats for your pet.
680. Make a special homemade toy for your pet.
681. Give a special bed or blanket to your pet.

682. Donate blankets or bedding to an animal shelter.
683. Carefully transport a spider or insect outside instead of squashing it.
684. Choose cruelty-free beauty and bath products.
685. Carry extra water and pet treats in your car.
686. Volunteer with an animal transport organization to help transport animals to shelters or unite pets with adopters.
687. Train your dog to become a certified therapy dog and visit nursing homes, veterans homes, hospitals, and domestic abuse shelters.
688. Surprise your pet with a new toy.
689. Set up a hummingbird feeder in your yard.
690. Donate toys to an animal shelter.
691. Spend extra time petting an animal you love.
692. Sing a song to your pet.
693. Shower your pet with compliments.

694. Help care for someone else's pets.
695. Put out a bird bath.
696. Volunteer at an animal shelter.
697. Volunteer or donate to a horse sanctuary or rescue center.
698. Volunteer your time with a local therapy horse riding program.
699. Volunteer as a docent at your local zoo or wildlife center.
700. Donate pet food to an animal shelter.
701. Donate cat litter to an animal shelter.
702. Make a bird feeder.
703. Make a donation to an animal shelter in memory of an animal you loved.
704. Adopt an animal online.
705. Foster an animal.
706. Give a small bag of kibble to a homeless person with a dog.

707. Pick up dog poop at the park.
708. Go to a dog park and hand out gift certificates to a local pet store.
709. Pay for the person behind you in line at the pet store.
710. Pay someone else's vet bill.
711. Drop off cat or dog food at your local food bank.
712. Build a feral cat shelter for the cold winter months.
713. Help someone look for their lost pet.
714. Pull over if you see a dog running along the road, and help reunite them with their owner.
715. Care for a butterfly with a broken wing.
716. Make your windows safer for birds by turning out lights at night and using window tape or "zen curtains" during the day.
717. Create a "bee bath" by filling a shallow bowl with clean water and stones for the bees to land on and take a drink.

718. Sponsor a beehive through an organization like The Bee Conservancy.

719. Provide a home for mason bees in your garden by purchasing or making a "bee condo" that has small tubes for the bees to live in.

720. Support your local beekeepers by buying local honey and beeswax products.

721. Choose to purchase bird-friendly, shade-grown coffee.

722. Install a nest box for birds.

723. Instead of scattering bread for the birds (which can make them ill), go to the park or fountain and scatter seeds and dried oats for the birds.

724. Buy a Migratory Bird Hunting and Conservation Stamp (or "Duck Stamp") to support National Wildlife Refuges.

725. Support accredited aquariums and zoos.

726. Report animal cruelty to the police if you witness an animal being abused or neglected.

727. Sponsor a doghouse to help provide shelter for an outdoor dog.

728. Lobby your city council to consider dog-chaining bans or restrictions.

729. Ask your local school to stop dissecting animals in its classrooms and to use a computer program or app such as Froggipedia instead.

730. Respect wildlife by observing them at a distance.

731. Read a book written about an animal or that imagines the perspective of an animal.

732. Make emergency plans for your pets in the event of a natural disaster.

Kind Acts while Traveling

"A good deed doesn't just evaporate and disappear. Its consequences saturate the universe and the goodness that happens somewhere, anywhere, helps in the transfiguration of the ugliness."

—Desmond Tutu

733. Bring small trinkets from your hometown, state, or country to give to people you encounter during your travels.

734. Post a note in the airport bathroom with words of encouragement for a stranger.

735. Offer to share your gum or hard candy with the person sitting next to you on the airplane during takeoff and landing.

736. Write a thank-you note for a flight attendant.

737. If you are traveling to a country with a different language, learn at least a few phrases in that language.

738. If you speak a foreign language, offer to translate for someone.

739. Help someone with their luggage.

740. Let someone go ahead of you in line.

741. Be patient.

742. Pay for someone else's snack.

743. Give someone else your seat.

744. Let someone borrow your phone charger.

745. Let someone borrow your phone to make a call.

746. Smile at everyone you meet.

747. Buy a bus or train ticket for someone.
748. Give a warm drink to a tollbooth worker.
749. Switch seats so a family can sit together.
750. Switch seats so someone else can have an aisle or window seat.
751. Leave a big tip.
752. Offer to take a photo of someone.
753. Applaud a street performer and drop money in their hat.
754. Research local charities in the places you will be traveling and donate your money or time.
755. Ask questions and listen to the experiences of others.
756. Joyfully do an activity that someone else wants to do, even if it's not your thing.
757. Buy a souvenir for someone.
758. Send a postcard to someone back home.

759. Pay for carbon offsets for your air travel emissions.
760. When you visit a museum, compliment a docent about their tour and share the highlights of what you learned.
761. Sit on a bench and people-watch. Send a good thought to everyone you see.
762. Pick up any litter you notice.
763. Flag a taxi for someone.
764. When browsing a bookstore, slip kind notes into the books.
765. When browsing a market, pay for someone else's purchase.
766. Leave a rave review of a restaurant, museum, or tourist location.
767. Donate a book to your hotel's common area or to a local library.
768. Leave a thank-you note for the housekeeper.
769. Exchange contact information with new friends

and follow up with a kind note or letter.

770. Leave every place you visit exactly as it was—or even better than you found it.

771. When you leave a foreign country, give someone else your spare change.

772. If you have extra rides left on your public transportation card, give it to someone else who could use it.

773. Surprise the hotel staff with flowers, cookies, or coffee.

774. Leave your guidebook in your hotel room for the next guest to use.

775. Donate your airline miles.

Kind Acts
While Shopping

"Spread love everywhere you go . . . Let no one ever come to you without leaving better and happier."

—*Mother Teresa*

776. Collect shopping carts from a parking lot and return them.
777. Compliment a salesperson to their manager.
778. Ask a salesperson for their opinion.
779. After trying on clothes, carefully refold the items you decide not to buy and put them back where you found them.
780. Let someone go ahead of you in line.

781. Leave an extra-generous tip.
782. Put loose change in a parking meter that is about to expire.
783. If someone ahead of you at the cash register is short a few cents, pay the difference for them.
784. Give coupons you don't need to other shoppers.
785. Offer to bag your own groceries.
786. Ask the checker what their favorite candy bar is—then buy it and give it to them.
787. Surprise the checker with a cold iced tea or soda.
788. Ask the checker how their day is going.
789. Help someone reach an item on a tall shelf.
790. Help someone lift a heavy item into their cart.
791. If a pantry staple is on sale, buy a few extra and drop them off at the local food bank.
792. Buy the ugliest produce (it all tastes the same!) and leave the pretty produce for the next person.

793. Pay for the groceries of the person behind you in line.

794. Buy a gift card and ask the checker to give it to a random shopper as a surprise.

795. Buy a balloon and ask the checker to give it to a child that passes through the line.

796. Slip kind notes and coupons into empty shopping baskets.

797. Wipe down your cart with a disinfecting wipe before you leave.

798. Write five-star reviews of your favorite local shops.

799. At the farmers market, buy an extra bouquet of flowers and give it to the cashier.

800. Compliment the farmer on their beautiful produce.

801. If it is a store you visit regularly, learn the workers' names. Greet them by name.

802. Say, "Thank you!" with a warm smile.

803. Give your cart or basket to someone entering the store.

804. Let someone else have the close parking spot.

805. At the post office, buy an extra book of stamps and give it to the person behind you in line.

806. Give the post office clerk a sweet drink or snack.

807. Take a couple of minutes to fill out the survey at the bottom of the receipt.

808. At a restaurant, clean up your table after you are done.

809. Offer to bus someone else's table at a restaurant.

810. Hand over a kind note along with your money when you pay.

Online Kindness

"Always try to be a little kinder than is necessary."

—*James M. Barrie*

811. Add an inspiring quote to your email signature.
812. Use an uplifting image or quote as your social media background.
813. Leave an encouraging comment on someone's blog post.
814. Organize a "boost" where a bunch of people all leave encouraging comments and share someone's blog post or social media post.

815. Write a five-star review for a podcast you love.
816. Send an email of gratitude to someone. (Bonus points: CC their boss!)
817. Write a recommendation for someone on LinkedIn.
818. Share someone else's post on social media.
819. Send an email to your coworkers with a funny GIF and a kind note.
820. Share a heartwarming article on social media.
821. Listen to others.
822. Ask permission before you post a photo of someone on social media.
823. Send an email to say, "I appreciate you."
824. Respond to a curt email with grace and kindness.
825. Send an email of encouragement to someone.
826. Read over that email once more before sending to make sure your tone comes across as you intend.
827. Send a friend a link to an online playlist you made for them.

828. Send someone a helpful article that made you think of them.
829. Email a voice message telling someone, "You're doing a great job!"
830. Share helpful advice in an online forum.
831. Write a five-star review for a product or service you love.
832. Click the button to "like" positive, helpful online reviews.
833. Use a search engine like Amazon Smile to raise money for charity while you shop.
834. Search the web using Ecosia, a search engine that uses advertising revenue to plant trees around the world, or Rapusia, a search engine that donates profits to social and environmental projects.
835. Share a friend's campaign on social media.
836. Share an uplifting or informative email newsletter that you love.

837. Send an email to someone about how their work impacted you.
838. Reach out to an old friend on social media to reconnect.
839. Offer a helpful recommendation when someone crowdsources information on social media.
840. Post a beautiful photograph, art piece, poem, or creative gift you have made for others to enjoy for free online.

Medical Kindness

"Sometimes it takes only one act of kindness and caring to change a person's life."

—*Jackie Chan*

841. Donate blood.
842. Join the bone marrow registry.
843. Sign up to be an organ donor.
844. Donate coloring books and crayons to a pediatrician's waiting room.
845. Donate magazines and books to a doctor's waiting room.

846. Next time you have an appointment, bring a homemade treat for the staff at your doctor or dentist's office.

847. Ask the receptionist how their day is going.

848. Look your doctor in the eye and say, "Thank you for all you have done for me. I appreciate you."

849. Write rave reviews of your doctors online.

850. Compliment a nurse/technician to their supervisor.

851. Decorate cards and drawings of thanks and drop them off at the front desk of the hospital for the heroes who work there.

852. Donate stuffed animals to the children's hospital.

853. Bring coffee and bagels to the nurse's station at the hospital.

854. Send a heartfelt card thanking a doctor or nurse for their help.

855. Grow out your hair and donate it to an organization like Locks of Love.

856. If you are a breastfeeding mother, donate your extra breastmilk through your local milk bank.
857. Donate masks or medical supplies to your local hospital.
858. Knit a blanket, hat, or booties and donate them to preemies in the NICU.
859. Make care packages with tissues, unscented lotion, hand sanitizer, and travel toiletries to give to parents of NICU babies in the hospital.
860. Host a fundraiser drive for a medical cause you care about.
861. Bring a hot meal to the hospital chaplain to thank them for their care.
862. Bring a hot meal to someone whose relative is in the hospital.
863. Drive someone to a medical appointment.
864. Volunteer as a candy striper at the hospital.
865. Volunteer at a medical testing center.

866. Donate to a fundraising page to help pay for someone's medical expenses.

867. Organize a blood drive in your community.

868. Donate menstrual supplies to a women's shelter.

869. Make a postpartum care package for someone who recently gave birth.

870. Create or join a "meal train" for someone who recently underwent surgery or other major medical treatment.

871. Create a well-stocked first aid kit and bring it with you—to the zoo, the park, the soccer game. You never know when someone might need a Band-Aid or an ice pack!

872. Donate to a charity, such as Doctors Without Borders, that provides medical supplies to developing countries.

873. Volunteer to prepare a meal at a local Ronald McDonald House, an organization that provides

free temporary housing near hospitals for families who need to travel for medical care.

374. Volunteer as a patient escort at a medical clinic.

375. Send a card to someone who can no longer attend community events due to illness.

376. Offer to watch someone's children or pets if they need to go to a medical appointment.

377. Volunteer to play music or put on a puppet show at a children's hospital.

378. Volunteer to lead a craft activity at a children's hospital.

379. Bring cards and treats to the doctors and nurses working in the Emergency Room.

380. If you see Emergency Medical Technicians (EMTs) out and about, thank them for what they do.

381. Pay for the coffee or meal of an EMT, doctor, or nurse in uniform or scrubs.

882. Sew and donate "activity mats" or "busy blankets" for patients with Alzheimer's disease or dementia.

883. Volunteer to teach lessons in arts or athletics through CoachArt, a national organization that matches volunteer coaches with children impacted by chronic illness.

884. Volunteer to help grant wishes for children with critical illnesses through an organization like the Make a Wish Foundation.

885. Serve as a hospice volunteer, providing comfort and support for patients and their families.

886. Take part in a community event like the Walk to End Alzheimer's or the Relay for Life to honor survivors, caregivers, and those lost to cancer.

Neighborhood Kindness

"I've learned that people will forget what you said, people will forget what you did, but people will never forget how you made them feel."

—Maya Angelou

887. Surprise your neighbor with homemade cookies.
888. Bring in your neighbor's garbage and recycling bins from the curb.
889. Pick up litter around your neighborhood.
890. Compliment a neighbor's dog.
891. Pick up after your dog.
892. Rake a neighbor's leaves.

893. Bring a neighbor's newspaper up to their front step.
894. Instead of hurrying inside your house, pause for a few minutes to chat with your neighbor.
895. Offer to bring in a neighbor's mail and packages when they are out of town.
896. Share your garden's bounty with your neighbors.
897. Ask a neighbor, "How are you doing?" And really listen.
898. Invite your neighbor to a backyard barbecue.
899. Help your neighbor look for their lost pet.
900. On September 28, National Good Neighbor Day, give your neighbor a card to thank them for being a good neighbor.
901. Ask your neighbor for advice or recommendations.
902. Introduce your neighbor to your pets.
903. Offer to babysit for your neighbor.

04. Always drive slowly and carefully through your neighborhood.

05. Leave a note in a neighbor's mailbox complimenting their front yard.

06. Give your neighbor your phone number so they can contact you if there is an emergency or they need your help for any reason.

07. Offer to pet-sit for your neighbor if they go out of town.

08. After you sweep your driveway, sweep your neighbor's driveway too.

09. After you wash your car, wash your neighbor's car too.

10. Observe quiet hours and be considerate about noise.

11. Ask your neighbor about the flowers in their yard.

12. Tie a balloon to your neighbor's mailbox on their birthday.

913. Shovel your neighbor's walkway after it snows.
914. Mow your neighbor's lawn after you mow your own.
915. Give a coupon to your neighbor.
916. Offer to let your neighbor put extra recycling or trash in your bins.
917. Smile and wave hello.
918. Alert your neighbor that a package was delivered to their doorstep.
919. Offer to water your neighbor's plants when they are out of town.
920. Bring your neighbor flowers from your garden.
921. Ask your neighbor about their children or grandchildren.
922. Bring your neighbor groceries when they are sick.
923. Buy two-for-one specials at the grocery store and bring the extra to a neighbor.

024. Use sidewalk chalk to write encouraging messages in front of your house for neighbors to see.

025. Invite your neighbor to share a meal with you.

026. Organize a neighborhood block party.

Community Kindness

"Kindness can become its own motive. We are made kind by being kind."

—*Eric Hoffer*

927. Leave quarters on a laundry machine.
928. Donate canned goods to a food pantry.
929. Deliver baked goods to a fire station.
930. Donate a copy of your favorite book to the library.
931. Pay for a stranger's public transportation.
932. Paint a mural in your town.

933. Pick up litter.
934. Volunteer at a soup kitchen.
935. Buy someone else's cup of coffee or tea.
936. Give a sandwich to someone in need.
937. Donate toiletries to a homeless shelter.
938. Visit a cemetery and leave flowers for a stranger.
939. Donate your old cell phone or other electronics.
940. Go to your favorite bookstore and slip dollar bills between the pages of books.
941. Volunteer to build a house with Habitat for Humanity.
942. Donate an old pair of shoes.
943. Donate diapers and feminine products to a women's shelter.
944. Donate baby food to a homeless shelter.
945. Sign a petition for a local cause.
946. Leave a kind note in a public bathroom.

947. Surprise your hairdresser with flowers or chocolates

948. Attend your local city council meeting and thank someone for their service.

949. Write a thank-you letter to the mayor, or to another local elected official.

950. Write a letter to the editor of your local newspaper praising an unsung hero in your community.

951. Drop by the local newsroom with coffee and bagels for the staff and reporters.

952. Contact the local news station about a positive news story in your community.

953. Decorate a bus stop with flowers and balloons.

954. Join a volunteer organization in your community.

955. Host a screening of a documentary you care about.

56. Ask the librarian if there are any overdue fees on other accounts and pay them off as a kind surprise.

57. If you are fluent in another language, volunteer as an English-language tutor.

58. Leave a treat in your mailbox with a note of thanks for your mail carrier.

59. Offer sunscreen to others when you are outside on a sunny day.

60. Offer to take a photo of someone or a group of people who are struggling to take a selfie together.

61. Venture slightly out of your comfort zone to make someone smile.

62. Help weed, plant, and maintain a community garden.

963. Offer to tutor a student in your community.
964. Host a book club in your community featuring a book that fosters connection, opens minds, and sparks conversation.
965. Volunteer to help a local organization fundraise and apply for grants.
966. Join the board of a local nonprofit.
967. Volunteer as an usher or ticket seller for your local community theater.
968. Work the information booth at your local farmers market.
969. Help set up or clean up a community fair or event.
970. Volunteer at a community cleanup or city beautification event.
971. Take part in a local road race to raise money for charity or support a cause you care about.

972. Volunteer as a docent at a local museum.

973. Hold a community book drive and donate books to the library, a school, or an organization like the Boys & Girls Club.

974. Hold a coat drive to collect warm winter coats for those who need them.

975. Volunteer as a greeter at a community center, senior center, play, or local event.

National & Global Kindness

"Kindness is the light that dissolves all walls between souls, families, and nations."

—*Paramahansa Yogananda*

976. Send a care package to someone in the military.
977. Buy a meal or drink for someone in military uniform.
978. Write a letter to your representative thanking them for an action they have taken on your behalf.
979. Send thank-you cards to the troops through an organization like Operation Gratitude.
980. Mail care packages to families of deployed soldiers.

981. Volunteer to help people register to vote.

982. Volunteer to be a poll worker on election day.

983. Plant a tree in a national forest through an organization such as A Living Tribute.

984. Help global reforestation efforts by donating to organizations such as One Tree Planted or The Nature Conservancy.

985. Leave a glowing five-star review for a book you loved.

986. Reach out to an artist whose work touches you.

987. Nominate your favorite podcast for an award.

988. Write an empowering poem and share it with the world.

989. Volunteer as a business mentor for small business owners around the world through an organization such as MicroMentor or Dream Mentorship.

990. Be part of a book launch team to spread the word about a new book coming into the world.

991. Compile the positive reviews of a book from Amazon or Goodreads and email them to the author.

992. Email a role model to tell them about the impact they have had on your life.

993. Sign a petition for a cause you care about.

994. Donate to a charity working across the world from where you live.

995. Host a foreign exchange student.

996. Volunteer as a "decoy" for dogs in training with the TSA Explosives Detection K-9 program at your closest airport.

997. Donate your old eyeglasses to Lions Clubs International.

998. Donate a farm animal to someone across the globe through an organization such as Heifer International.

999. Donate to help build a well for a community in a developing country through an organization like Lifewater International.

1000. For your birthday, instead of asking for gifts, ask for donations to a nonprofit organization.

1001. Celebrate World Kindness Day on November 13 every year.

Additional Kindness Quotes

"You cannot do a kindness too soon, for you never know how soon it will be too late."

—Ralph Waldo Emerson

"When you feel grateful for something, you notice what it needs and you do what you can to take care of it."

—Kristi Nelson

"For every atom belonging to me as good belongs to you."

—Walt Whitman

"Remember that the happiest people are not those getting more, but those giving more."

—H. Jackson Brown Jr.

"Understanding that you matter inspires gratitude and loving action."

—Deborah Ramelli

"Kindness in words creates confidence. Kindness in thinking creates profoundness. Kindness in giving creates love."

—Lao Tzu

"Trust allows you to give. Giving is abundant. As you give so it shall be given to you."

—Gary Zukav

About the Author

Dallas Woodburn is an award-winning author, podcast host, and book coach who helps women around the world write and publish the books inside their hearts. She is the author of seven books including *Your Book Matters: 52 Love Notes from My Creative Heart to Yours* and *The Best Week That Never Happened*, and her stories and essays have appeared in *The Los Angeles Times, Modern Loss, Chicken Soup for the Soul*, and many others. A former John Steinbeck Fellow in Creative Writing, Dallas has been honored with the Jefferson Award for public service, the international Glass Woman Prize, and four

Pushcart Prize nominations. She once spent an entire year doing a unique act of kindness every week and chronicling the journey on her blog. Dallas lives in California with her husband and two young daughters.

About Familius

Visit our website: www.familius.com

Familius is a global trade publishing company that publishes books and other content to help families be happy. To that end, we publish books for children and adults that invite families to live the Familius Ten Habits of Happy Families: love together, play together, learn together, work together, talk together, heal together, read together, eat together, give together,and laugh together. Founded in 2012, Familius is located in Sanger, California.

Connect

Facebook: www.facebook.com/familiusbooks
TikTok: @familiusbooks
YouTube: @Familius
Instagram: @familiusbooks

FAMILIUS

Helping families be happy.